W9-BLS-649
DuSable
Ed DeBevic's
Frango Mints
Ice Skating
Jazz
NAVY PIER
Navy Pier
Orchestra
Pedway
Pedway
Swans
Tiffany Lamp
eXchange
I ♡ IAN
J.T.B III
MAY
HI MOM
BEVIN
THE BURNS
♡ HSZ ♡
TTON
GIANT
JOUR
Yellow Bricks
Martha
Zschock
Zschock

Art Deco
Bike
Chicagoween
Gangster
Hardy Soul
Kids and Kites Festival
Lincoln Park Conservatory
Mayor
Quaker Oats
OLD FASHIONED
QUAKER OATS
Rainbow Cone
University of Chicago
Violets
Wrigley's Gum
WRIGLEY'S
DOUBLEMINT
CHEWING GUM

Journey Around

Chicago

from A to Z

Martha Day Zschock

COMMONWEALTH EDITIONS
Carlisle, Massachusetts

Designed by Heather Zschock

Commonwealth Editions
An imprint of Applewood Books, Inc.
Carlisle, MA 01741
Visit us at www.commonwealtheditions.com

Visit Martha Zschock at www.journeyaround.com

ISBN-13: 9781889833859

The Maxwell Street Blues Bus Production, pictured on the "V" page, is produced by the Maxwell Street Foundation and features "And This Was Free" street theatre with the Reverend John Johnson's original *Blues Bus* and blues music sets arranged by Mr. H Baron of the Blues.

10 9 8 7 6 5

Printed in Korea

To my wonderful family

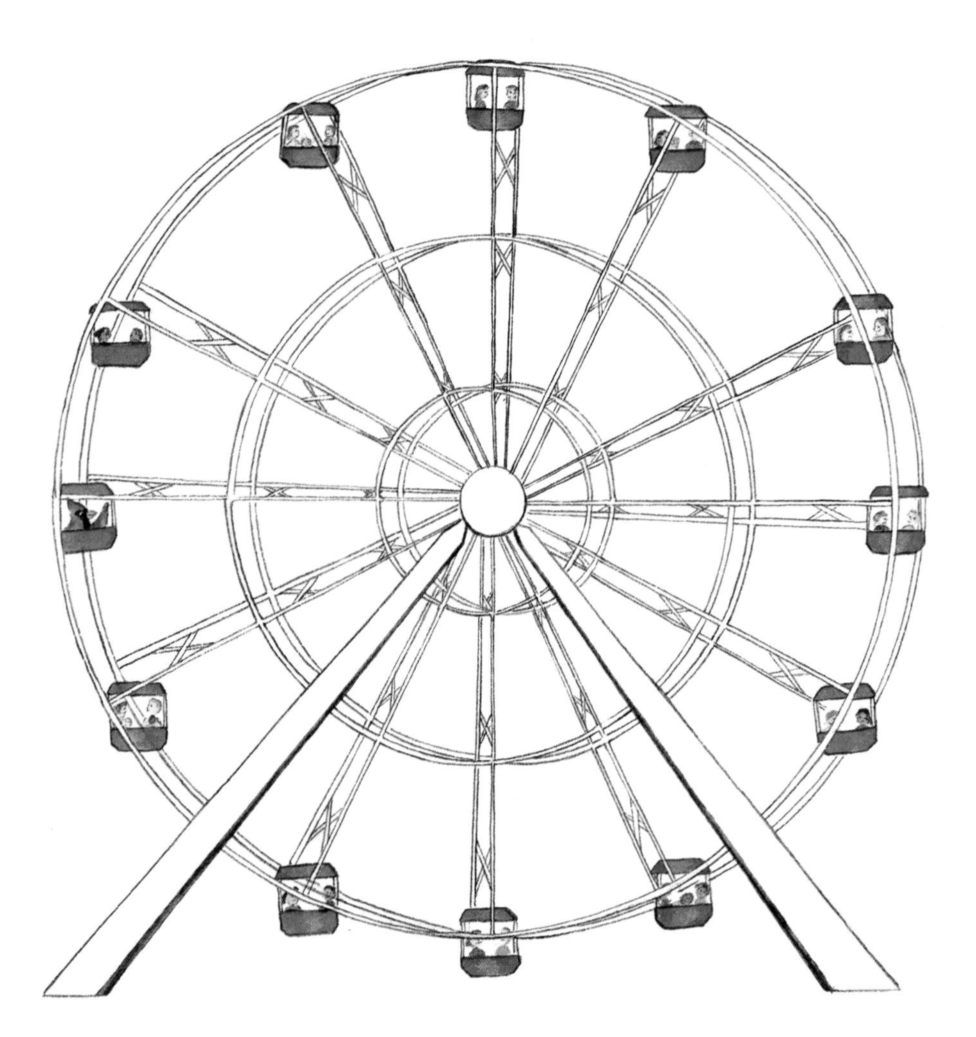

and to
the dedicated folks who make the city
of Chicago second to none!

A special thank you to . . . the "journey crew" at Commonwealth Editions, Stephanie Bowen, Elizabeth Muller, our friends at Jay's, our family in Chicago (Caroline and Michael Burns and Linda and Bill Gantz), and Dr. James Meserow and his son. In addition, many thanks to helpful friends at the Chicago Historical Society, Chicago Office of Tourism, City of Chicago's Department of Cultural Affairs, Friends of the Chicago River, Field Museum, Chicago Tribune, *Notebaert Nature Museum, Art Institute of Chicago, Jane Addams Hull-House Museum, Chicago Children's Choir, Polish Museum of America, Swedish American Museum Center, Lincoln Park Zoo, Marshall Field's, Frank Lloyd Wright Preservation Trust, DuSable Museum, Bronzeville Children's Museum, Naper Settlement, Chicago Public Library, Pizzeria Uno, Maxwell Street Foundation, Cut Rate Blues Band, Blues Kids of America, Museum of Science and Industry, and Museum Campus.*

Chicago, Chicago . . .

I'll show you around!

Greetings, my friends, and

Welcome to Chicago!

THE CITY OF CHICAGO rises majestically from the shoreline of Lake Michigan, which stretches east of the city with its ocean-like expanse. Chicago is the "hub" of the Midwest, America's third largest city, and an ever-evolving work of art!

It's hard to imagine today that the bustling city of Chicago was once a marshy area the Native Americans called "Checagou" ("land of the wild onion"). Because its location provided a natural gateway to the Midwest, Chicago was destined to become a major shipping port. With the opening of the Erie Canal, which linked the Atlantic Ocean to the Great Lakes, and a shipping canal linking the Great Lakes to the Mississippi River, Chicago's population boomed as immigrants from all over the world arrived seeking opportunity in the Midwest.

The early settlers were a hardy bunch, establishing new lives on an unfamiliar prairie. Their determination and faith sowed the seeds for the dynamic, bustling city that Chicago is today. Undeterred by weather, a major fire, and economic setbacks, Chicagoans have earned the right to proudly boast their many firsts, biggests, and bests. Though called the "Second City," Chicago is second to none!

Come, there's much to explore. Let's take a journey around Chicago!

Lincoln Park
Old Town
Lake Michigan
Gold Coast
Magnificent Mile
Near North Side
River North
North Branch
Streeterville
Navy Pier
Chicago River
The Loop
Greek Town
Chicago Harbor
N
Grant Park
W
E
South Branch of Chicago River
South Loop
Near West Side
S
Chicago
Chinatown
Near South Side and Hyde Park

THANKS TO ITS PUBLIC ART PROGRAM, Chicago is graced with an impressive collection of outdoor sculptures. A 1978 city law requires that a percentage of costs for building and renovating municipal buildings be set aside to purchase works of art. Is it a cow, a woman, or a baboon? The untitled Picasso statue was not well received at first, but it is now a beloved symbol of the city.

The Museum of Contemporary Art invites the curious to view works of modern art created since 1945.

Main: *Flamingo*, Federal Center
Inset: Picasso statue, Richard J. Daley Plaza
Detail: Museum of Contemporary Art

CHICAGO BECAME THE HUB of the Northwest Territory in the 1840s when a new canal linked the Great Lakes to the Mississippi River. The huge increase of activity polluted the Chicago River, the city's primary source of fresh water. Engineers addressed the problem in 1900 by reversing the river's flow away from the lake. Today, forty-five movable bridges accommodate traffic both on and off the river.

Main: Chicago River
Inset: Drawbridge gears, River Museum, Michigan Avenue Bridge Tower
Detail: Centennial Fountain

Friends of the Chicago River work diligently to clean up the river and revitalize the surrounding area. Join them in the spring for Chicago River Day!

Commuter trains circle Chicago's center.

CHICAGO'S ELEVATED TRAIN, the "L" or "El," circles "The Loop," Chicago's central business district. Often noisy, but always scenic, the cars have carried passengers above Wabash, Van Buren, Wells, and Lake Streets for over a hundred years. The cost of a ride has increased from five cents in the early 1900s to close to two dollars today. The Chicago Transit Authority (CTA) operates six commuter lines in the city.

Children can board the city's first steam engine, the Pioneer, at the Chicago Historical Society.

Main: The "L"
Inset: Train map, the Loop
Detail: Pioneer, Chicago Historical Society

SINCE THE ARRIVAL OF SUE, the world's largest and most complete *Tyrannosaurus rex* skeleton, attendance has soared at the Field Museum. Upholding the museum's mission to serve both the public and science, Sue is displayed using steel brackets that allow researchers to remove bones for study. Young paleontologists can dig for dinosaur bones at the Chicago Children's Museum.

The Field Museum has six acres of exhibits featuring specimens from cultures and environments around the world.

The Chicago Children's Museum boasts three floors of hands-on exhibits for curious kids.

Main: Sue, Field Museum
Inset: Chicago Children's Museum, Navy Pier
Detail: Museum exhibits

SINCE *THE DEMOCRAT* ROLLED OFF THE PRESSES IN 1833, Chicago has had over 450 newspapers reflecting the diverse interests of its citizens. The two most popular Chicago newspapers today are the *Tribune* and the *Sun-Times*. The majestic Tribune Tower has stones from historic sites around the world embedded in its base: Look for pieces of the Taj Mahal, the pyramids of Egypt, and the Alamo. It also has a moon rock!

Chicago's historic Printers Row attracts over 75,000 people to its annual book fair.

Main: Tribune Tower and Wrigley Building
Inset: Extra! Extra! Read all about it!
Detail: Printers Row Book Fair

Farmers flocked to fertile fields.

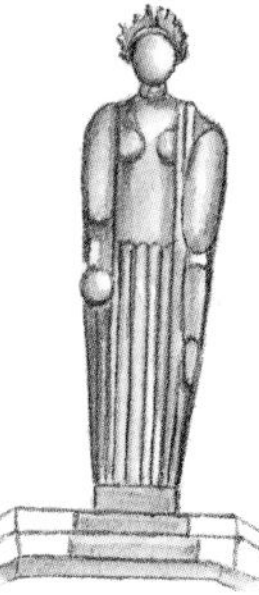

EARLY PIONEERS SETTLED IN WOODED RIVER AREAS that provided a plentiful supply of fresh water and trees for building and heating homes. Plowing prairie fields was difficult until 1837, when John Deere designed a steel plow that efficiently sliced through the thick layers of sod. The rich Illinois soil was well suited to cultivating crops. As farm goods were shipped to the East, Chicago became a boomtown.

Main: Farm-in-the-Zoo, Lincoln Park
Inset: Notebaert Nature Museum
Detail: *Ceres,* Chicago Board of Trade

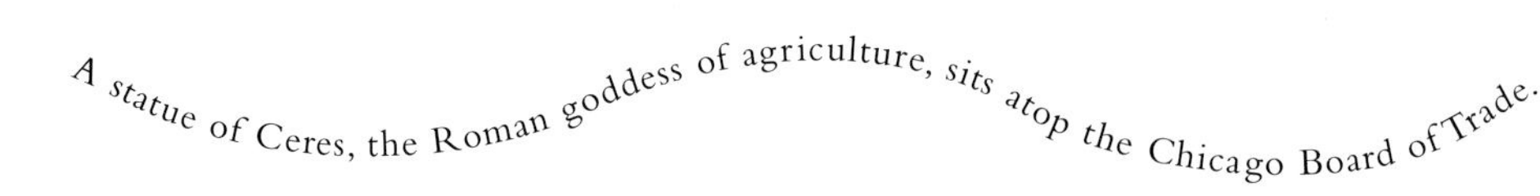

A statue of Ceres, the Roman goddess of agriculture, sits atop the Chicago Board of Trade.

Games guide kids through galleries.

THE ART INSTITUTE OF CHICAGO was founded in 1879 as both a museum and a school. Games, interactive videos, and programs provided in the Kraft Education Center help guide children through the extensive collections. Bronze lions guarding the entrance are decorated for the holidays. You may touch the lions, but please don't touch the art inside. Natural oils on your hands can damage artwork!

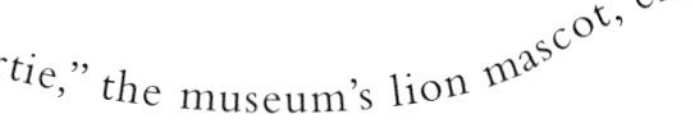

"Artie," the museum's lion mascot, encourages kids to explore the fascinating collections at the Art Institute of Chicago.

Main: Bronze lions, by Edward Kemeys
Inset: Illustration of *American Gothic*, originally by Grant Wood
Detail: Museum exhibits

Hurrah for the home teams!

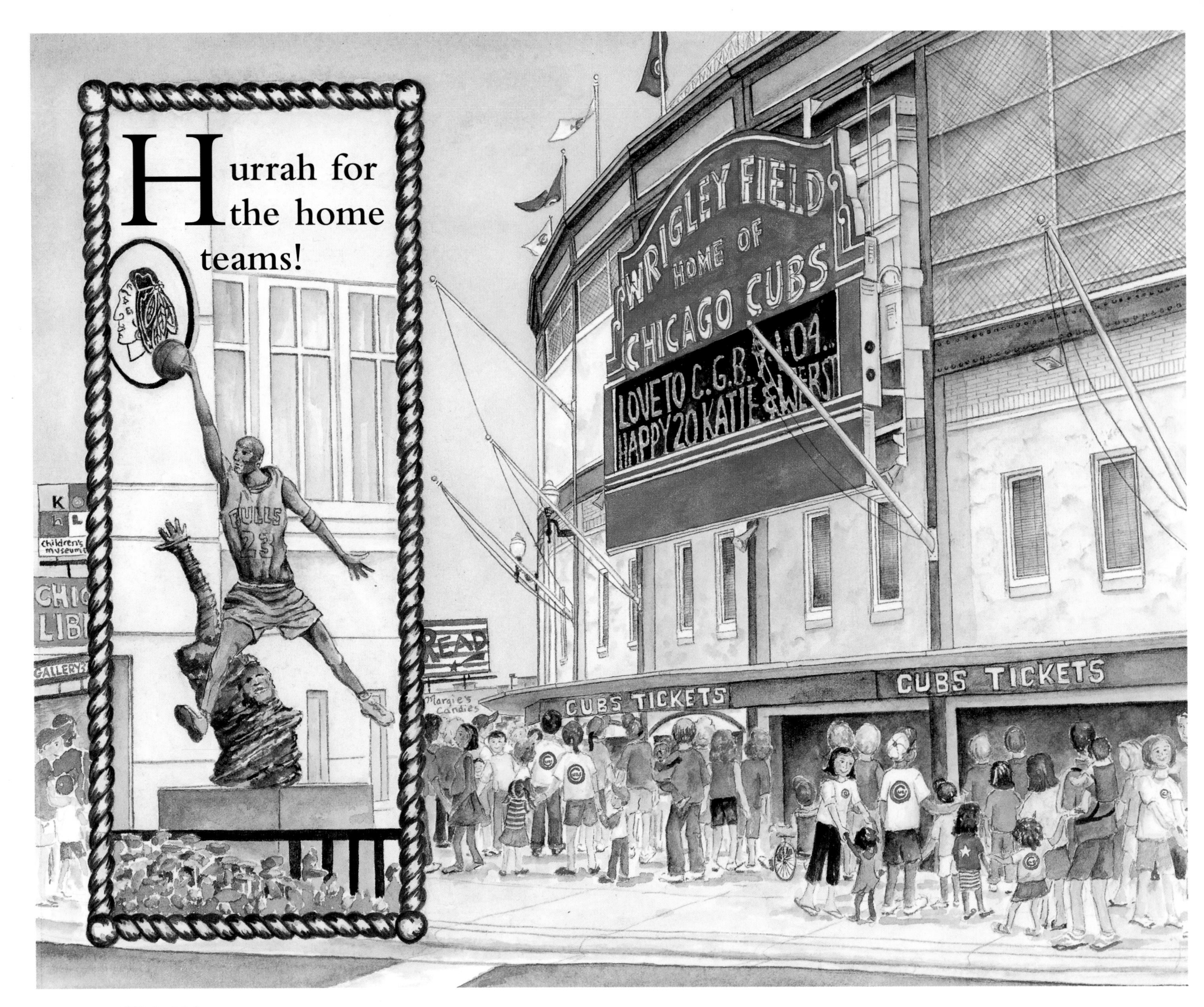

CHICAGOANS ARE ENTHUSIASTIC SUPPORTERS of their sports teams, win or lose. Although the Cubs haven't won the World Series since 1908, an afternoon at historic Wrigley Field is good old-fashioned fun, and there's always hope! Past and present sports heroes, such as Michael Jordan (Bulls) and Sammy Sosa (Cubs), have inspired young players to achieve their personal best.

Main: Wrigley Field
Inset: Michael Jordan statue, United Center
Detail: Hurrah for the home teams!

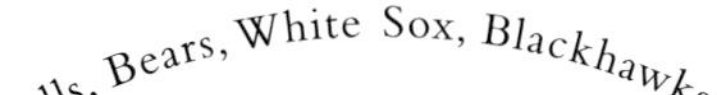

Bulls, Bears, White Sox, Blackhawks, and Cubs logos are practically worn as uniforms by loyal fans throughout the city.

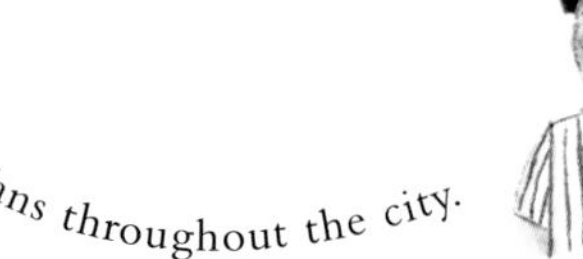

Illinois introduced ingenious inventions.

ILLINOIS IS THE BIRTHPLACE OF THE ZIPPER, the Tinker Toy, and the steel-framed skyscraper, as well as four-wheeled roller skates, vacuum cleaners, steel plows, and nuclear chain reactors. Fairs were once showcases for progress and the latest inventions. The Ferris wheel and the automatic dishwasher made their debut at the World's Columbian Exposition in 1893. The Ferris wheel at Navy Pier commemorates this fun invention.

Abraham Lincoln, who lived much of his life in Illinois, was the only U.S. president to hold a patent. In 1849, he designed a device to help buoy vessels over shallow water in rivers.

Main: Ferris wheel, Navy Pier
Inset: *Nuclear Energy*, University of Chicago
Detail: Abe Lincoln

SEEKING A BETTER LIFE, immigrants arrived in Chicago with little money and few possessions. Jane Addams established Hull House in 1889 to offer immigrants support services such as education and childcare. Her settlement house celebrated the immigrants' heritage and encouraged neighbors to help each other. Today, the city boasts many ethnic museums that celebrate Chicago's rich cultural diversity.

Main: Jane Addams Hull House, University of Illinois, Chicago Campus
Inset: A few of Chicago's many ethnic museums
Detail: Chicago Children's Choir

The Chicago Children's Choir provides musical opportunities for over 3,000 children from all races and cultures each year.

LINCOLN PARK ZOO WAS ESTABLISHED IN 1868 with the gift of a pair of swans from New York's Central Park. Now it has more than a thousand animals. A leader in research and education, the zoo is free and open to all 365 days a year. By creating natural habitats for animals, the Brookfield Zoo shows visitors realistic animal environments, such as spongy Illinois wetlands and the rainforests of South America, Africa, and Asia.

The Hamill Family Play Zoo at the Brookfield Zoo lets children explore nature in a kid-friendly way.

Main: Kangaroos, Brookfield Zoo
Inset: SBC Endangered Species Carousel, Lincoln Park Zoo
Detail: Hamill Family Play Zoo, Brookfield Zoo

IN THE 1800S, most of Chicago's buildings were wooden, making them perfect kindling for the devastating fire of 1871. The fire began on DeKoven Street when (some say) a cow kicked over a lantern in Mrs. O'Leary's barn. Fast-moving flames soon destroyed the downtown area. Only the stone Water Tower, the Chicago Avenue Pumping Station, and, strangely enough, Mrs. O'Leary's house remained! Today, the Chicago Fire Academy sits on the site of O'Leary's barn.

Main: Water Tower
Inset: *Pillar of Fire*, Chicago Fire Academy
Detail: "Cows on Parade" exhibit

Over the years, cows have become a symbol of the city. "Cows on Parade" was a colorful and hugely successful outdoor exhibit in 1999.

"ON STATE STREET, THAT GREAT STREET," as the song "Chicago" goes, Marshall Field built his famous department store in the late 1800s, "giving the lady what she wants" in an elegant setting. Other stores soon followed as famous merchants Richard Sears, Alvah Roebuck, and Carson Pirie Scott set up shop nearby. The stretch of Michigan Avenue just north of the river was nicknamed the "Magnificent Mile" as fancy stores, hotels, and restaurants moved in.

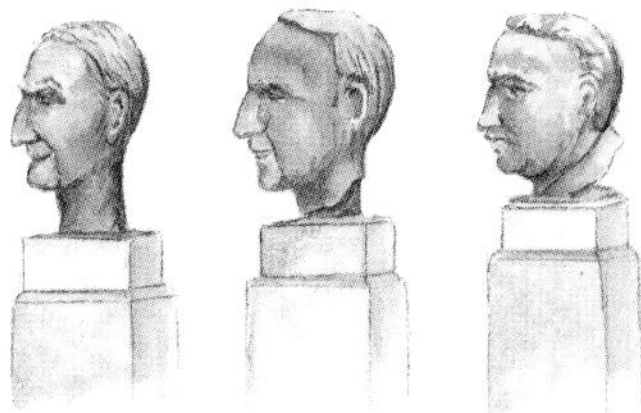

Outside the Merchandise Mart, the world's largest commercial building, the Merchant's Hall of Fame pays tribute to retail greats.

Main: Tiffany ceiling, Marshall Field's
Inset: Magnificent Mile, North Michigan Avenue
Detail: Merchant's Hall of Fame, Merchandise Mart

FRANK LLOYD WRIGHT developed his influential Prairie Style of architecture from his home and studio in nearby Oak Park. His low, flat building designs reflect the landscape of the Midwestern plains and are a sharp contrast to the Victorian houses that were popular in the late 1800s. Wright incorporated many elements of nature into his designs; tulip shapes graced stained-glass windows and a tree even grew right through his house!

Main: Frank Lloyd Wright Home and Studio, Oak Park
Inset: Frank Lloyd Wright window, Smith Museum of Stained Glass Windows
Detail: Lincoln Logs

Frank Lloyd Wright's son John invented Lincoln Logs. Building must run in the family!

AFTER THE CIVIL WAR, freed slaves were excluded from most jobs. With its fast-growing industries, Chicago was a place where they could find work. During the early 1900s, thousands flocked to the South Side, creating what became known as Black Metropolis, or Bronzeville. The DuSable Museum of African American History—named for Chicago's first settler, a Haitian fur trader—celebrates African Americans' experiences and achievements.

The Bronzeville Children's Museum and the Bronzeville Walk of Fame recognize notable African Americans who have lived in the area.

Main: Monument to the Great Northern Migration, Bronzeville Walk of Fame
Inset: DuSable Museum, South Side
Detail: Bronzeville Children's Museum and Walk of Fame

PIONEERS BEGAN SETTLING AREAS surrounding Chicago in the 1830s. Many made the dangerous journey to the prairie in covered wagons, which could hold up to two thousand pounds of supplies for the settlers' new lives. Families bought inexpensive parcels of land and set to work building homes, planting gardens, and making almost everything they needed from scratch.

Temporary log cabins soon were replaced by log houses that had chimneys and windows. Plank (instead of dirt) floors and a sleeping loft were considered luxuries.

Main: Covered wagon, Naper Settlement
Inset: Pioneer children's clothes
Detail: Log house, Swedish American Museum

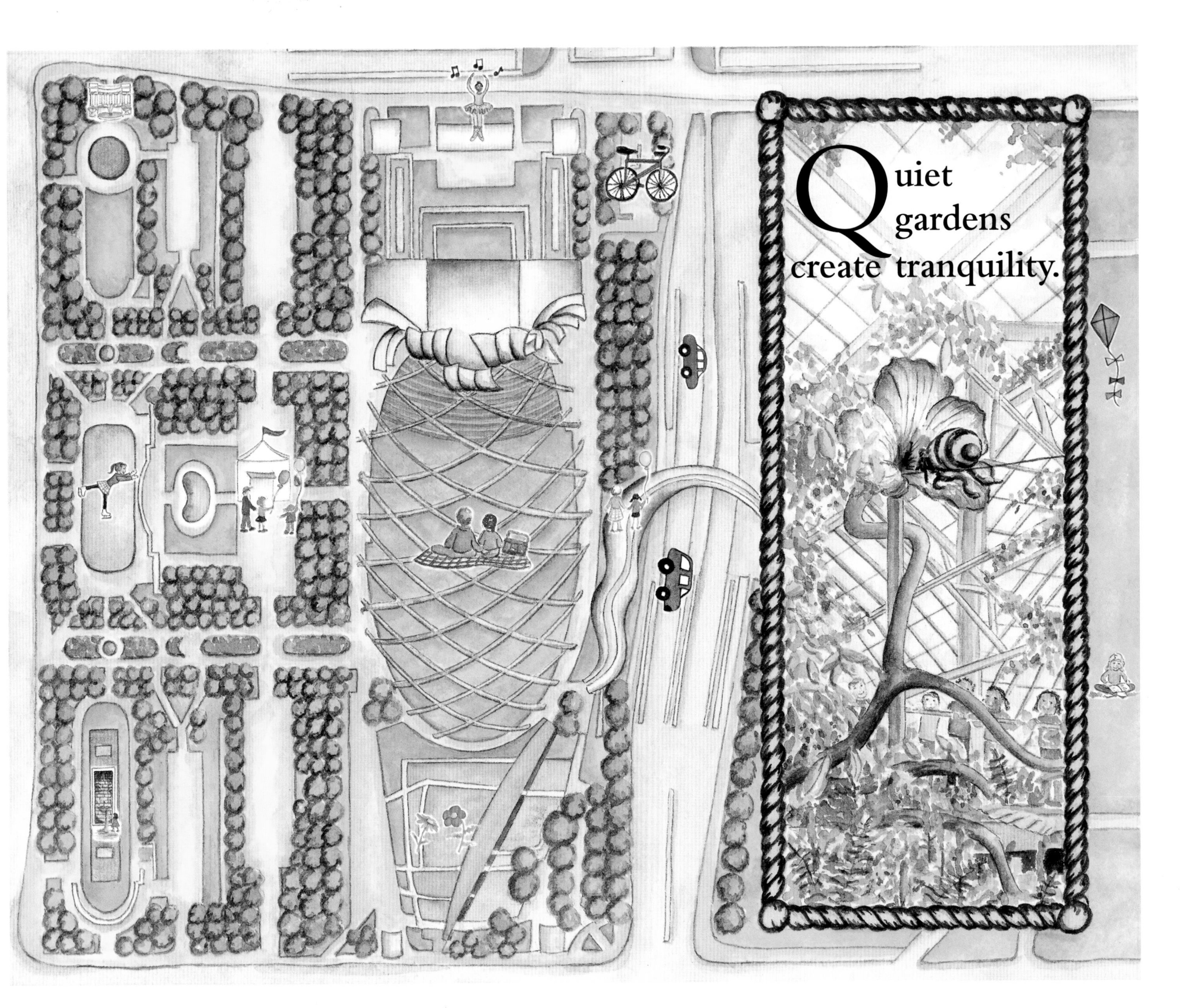

FROM ITS EARLIEST DAYS, Chicago has embraced the motto *Urbs in horto*, Latin for "City in a garden." Today the city boasts 7,300 acres of parkland, including gardens, conservatories, beaches, naturally landscaped areas, and even museums. The parks are a legacy of city planner Daniel Burnham and of farsighted citizens who lobbied in 1835 to keep Chicago's "front yard" clear of development. Millennium Park was created to celebrate Chicago's continuing legacy of innovation.

The chrysanthemum was designated the official flower of the city of Chicago in 1966.

Main: Millennium Park
Inset: Garfield Park Conservatory
Detail: Chrysanthemum, Chicago Botanic Garden

Reading reaps rich rewards.

THE CHICAGO PUBLIC LIBRARY, WITH ITS SEVENTY-NINE BRANCHES, hosts entertaining programs to encourage reading, writing, and learning. The Harold Washington Library Center is the world's largest public library building, with more than 2 million books and seventy miles of shelves. Chicago has been the home of many famous writers, including Shel Silverstein, Gwendolyn Brooks, and L. Frank Baum, author of *The Wizard of Oz*.

Main: Harold Washington Public Library
Inset: Tin Man, Oz Park
Detail: Storybook Dollhouse, Thomas Hughes Children's Library

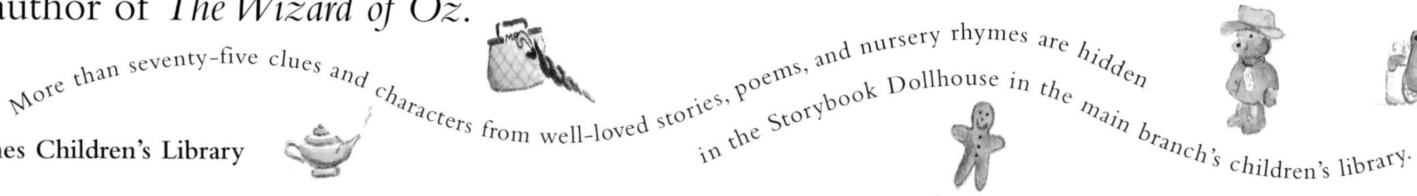

ARCHITECTS ENTHUSIASTIC ABOUT REBUILDING A CITY flocked to Chicago following the great fire of 1871. The invention of the elevator and the steel frame led to the "sky-scraper," and structures began to soar to astonishing heights. Building technology and styles advanced quickly, and Chicago soon became a museum of modern architecture. The Sears Tower is one of the world's ten tallest buildings.

Resting the weight of a building on a steel frame rather than on its walls allowed for larger windows.
"Chicago windows" have a large central pane and two smaller panes that open on each side.

Main: Bird's-eye view, John Hancock Center
Inset: Home Insurance Building, Chicago's first skyscraper, designed by William Jenney
Detail: "Chicago window"

Tasty treats tantalize the taste buds.

CHICAGO'S DIVERSE ETHNIC POPULATION offers a wide variety of delicious foods. Many old favorites have been redesigned with style—"Chicago style," that is. Deep-dish pizza originated here, and hot dogs are typically served with mustard, relish, onion, dill pickles, and tomatoes. Chicago is also famous for its thick steaks, rainbow ice cream, Wrigley's Gum, and Eli's cheesecake. The "Taste of Chicago" festival draws millions each summer.

In 1955, Ray Kroc founded McDonald's Corporation in nearby Des Plaines. Hot dogs are served '50s-style at Superdawg, and billions of Oreos are manufactured each year in Chicago. Have some for dessert!

Main: Pizzeria Uno
Inset: Taste of Chicago
Detail: McDonald's Museum, Des Plaines; Superdawg; Oreo

Upton Sinclair urged changes at Union Stock Yard.

IN 1865, THE UNION STOCK YARD WAS FORMED as a place to process and pack meat. Laborers slaughtered thousands of cows, hogs, and sheep each day for low wages in unsanitary conditions. Upton Sinclair's 1906 book *The Jungle* led to laws for the safe handling of food and helped improve conditions in the workers' "Back of the Yards" neighborhood.

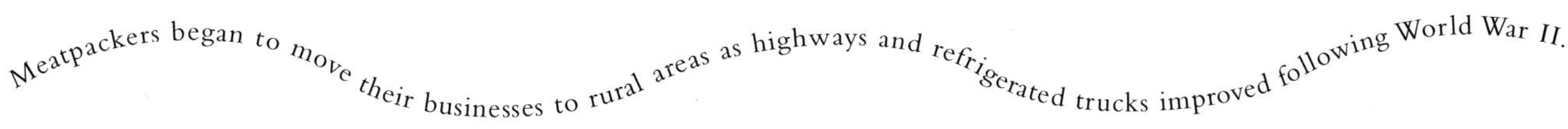

Main: Union Stock Yard gate, designed by Daniel Burnham
Inset: Children, "Back of the Yards"
Detail: Refrigerated truck

Voices vibrate with hope.

THE BLUES, a style of music that expresses both sadness and hope, grew from the chants of slaves working in the fields. African American musicians brought this soulful style to Chicago and cultivated it into an electrified sound that influenced jazz, rock, and gospel. Chicago's annual Blues Festival in Grant Park celebrates old favorites and welcomes new talent.

Main: "And This Was Free," *Maxwell Street Blues Bus Production* and the Cut Rate Blues Band
Inset: Chicago Blues Festival, Grant Park
Detail: Chess Records

Many blues legends began their careers as street musicians at the Maxwell Street Market and later moved to clubs. They gained worldwide recognition through recordings made at studios like Chess Records.

LAKE MICHIGAN, offering Chicago 29 miles of shoreline, defines the city's past, present, and future. The Great Lakes region provided native people and settlers with plentiful fresh water, game, and fertile soil. Today the lake is Chicago's main recreational area; boating, swimming, fishing, and lakeside strolling are favorite pastimes. Ongoing pollution prevention and cleanup efforts help safeguard the lake's future.

Buckingham Fountain's seahorses symbolize the four states that border Lake Michigan. This beautiful fountain is lit with a rainbow of color during the summer months.

Main: Chicago Lighthouse, off Navy Pier
Inset: Beach fun
Detail: Buckingham Fountain, Grant Park

REROUTING TRAFFIC HELPED CREATE MUSEUM CAMPUS, a 57-acre extension of Burnham Park in 1998. The project united three of Chicago's major scientific institutions with landscaped walkways and trolley service. Visitors can journey to distant planets at the Adler Planetarium, dive into the Amazon at the Shedd Aquarium, and explore natural history at the Field Museum—all in one day!

Main: Dolphin, Shedd Aquarium
Inset: StarRider Theater, Adler Planetarium
Detail: Amazon Rising, Shedd Aquarium; Henry Moore's sundial, Adler Planetarium

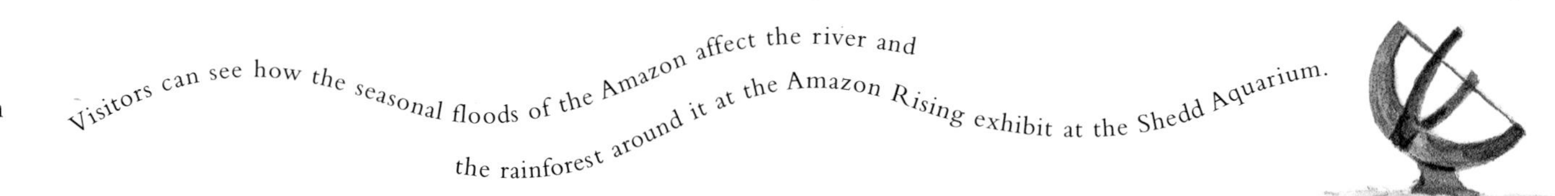

Young and old yell bravo!

CHICAGO HAS MANY OPTIONS FOR THEATER LOVERS. From Broadway plays to remakes of classic fairy tales, from symphony orchestras to world-class ballet, there's a performance to fit *any* interest. Many theaters offer special children's productions, often inviting the audience to meet the performers. During the summer, the Chicago Symphony Orchestra performs under the stars at Ravinia, an outdoor theater just north of the city.

The Chicago Cultural Center hosts programs throughout the year and introduces children to the stage during "Theater Fever" in February.

Main: Chicago Theater
Inset: Ravinia, Highland Park
Detail: A star is born

IN THE 1800S, AS THE POPULATION SKYROCKETED, Chicago became a hub of railroad transportation. In 1934, the Chicago, Burlington & Quincy Railroad christened the Pioneer Zephyr, a "shovelnose" train that broke speed records. Today Chicago is a hub of air travel, with more than 70 million people passing through O'Hare International Airport each year.

Main: Pioneer Zephyr, Museum of Science and Industry
Inset: O'Hare International Airport
Detail: Christmas tree ship

During the holidays in the late 1800s and early 1900s, Chicagoans looked forward to the arrival of "Christmas Tree ships" that carried trees from Wisconsin. They purchased their trees directly from the boats, which moored at the city's bridges.

DuSable
Ed DeBevic's
Frango Mints
Ice Skating
Jazz
NAVY PIER
Navy Pier
Orchestra
Pedway
Pedway
Swans
Tiffany Lamp
EXchange
I ♡ IAN
J.T.B III
MAY
HI MOM
BEVIN
THE BURNS
♡ HSZ ♡
TTON
GIANT
JOUR
Yellow Brick
Martha Zschock
Zschock

Art Deco
Bike
Chicagoween
Gangster
Hardy Soul
Kids and Kites Festival
Lincoln Park
Conservatory
Mayor
Quaker Oats
OLD FASHIONED
QUAKER
OATS
Rainbow Cone
University of
Chicago
Violets
Wrigley's Gum
WRIGLEY'S
DOUBLEMINT
CHEWING GUM